WHEELS OF CHANGE

A venerable, 75 year old bicycle manufacturer
tries to reinvent itself in the age of Artificial
Intelligence.
Was it successful?

Jee Va

ISBN-13: 9798389153769
ISBN-10: 1477123456

Cover design by: Art Painter
Library of Congress Control Number: 2018675309
Printed in the United States of America

To my dad who gave me the gift of writing and my mom who taught me the virtues of hard work and persistence.

The story, all names, characters, and incidents portrayed in this book are fictitious. No identification with actual persons (living or deceased), places, buildings, and products is intended or should be inferred. All opinions expressed in this book are the author's own.

CONTENTS

FOREWORD

The Age of Artificial Intelligence (AI) has arrived.

From self driving cars, garrulous ChatGPTs to uncanny deepfakes, we have all been exposed to AI (or have been reading about it) in recent days.

But it has also been invading our lives surreptitiously. Your email program automatically completes your sentences; the robot vacuum cleaner in your house deftly steers past obstacles; your mobile phone recognizes your face when you try to open it, your friendly voice assistant plays your favorite song every morning.

While all this is going on in the home front, the AI revolution has been happening at a much bigger scale in the corporate world. Examples are bots that can automate workflows, software that can analyze customer sentiment, intelligent robots that can do quality inspections in a factory, smart sensors that can predict equipment failure and so on.

With AI going mainstream, many companies are actively looking at how to incorporate AI into their business. Today it has become a key differentiator. Soon, it will become a necessity for survival.

However, transforming a traditional business to the age of AI is not easy. These companies have people, processes and systems equipped to solve problems differently, from a different era.

Business processes have to be changed, employees have to be retrained, systems have to be re engineered. In almost all these cases, the key driver is automation, which improves efficiency and reduces cost. In other cases, companies may have to redesign their products or services, to take advantage of AI. This helps them differentiate their products from competitors and increase sales.

Cozmo bicycles, est 1945.

It is a 75 year old company that finds itself right in the middle of the AI revolution. Faced with a young, nimble competitor who has captured the lead in many markets, Cozmo bicycles has to rapidly innovate in order to survive.

Wheels of Change is a fictional account of how this company grapples with these challenges and tries to reinvent itself. Along the way, the book introduces the reader to the basic concepts in AI and the promise and perils of introducing AI in the workplace.

This is not a technical book, even though it discusses many technical concepts. It is written in a light, conversational style and focuses more on the business issues faced while introducing AI in an organization.

Who is the audience for this book?

It is an entry level book for people new to AI. It highlights the people, process and technology challenges an organization will face as it reimagines itself for the Age of AI. Managers and non technical people who are embarking on an AI initiative in their company would find this book useful.

It gave me a lot of satisfaction and joy to narrate this in the form of a story. I hope you, the reader will find it enjoyable and useful.

Jee Va

March 31, 2023

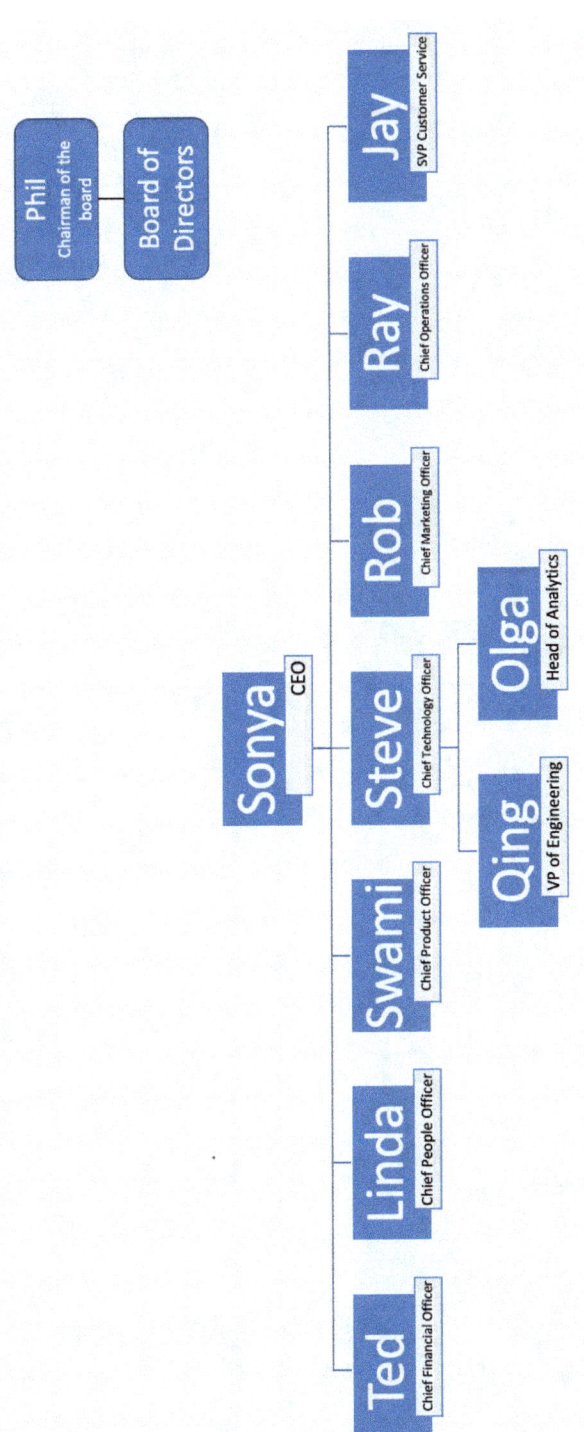

PART ONE

1. THE DAY OF RECKONING

March 1, 2022.

When CFO Ted ended his speech, the usual applause and cheers were missing. He had just presented the quarterly financial results of **Cozmo Bicycles** to the leadership team. There was a sobering silence as he walked back to his seat.

The last quarter was not very good for Cozmo Bicycles. Sales were down by 10% from last year. More importantly, they were losing to their competitors in almost all areas.

Cozmo Bicycles was established in 1945, by Sam Davidson. Initially they started manufacturing bicycles as an OEM (Original Equipment Manufacturer) and sold them exclusively under other brand names as a private label.

After about 40 years of doing business this way, Sam passed over the reins of the business to his son Phil. Phil was a bicycle aficionado in his own right, and boldly took the company to a new era. Under his leadership, Cozmo decided to establish its own brand of bicycles and go directly to consumers in North America and countries in Europe.

Their strategy worked very well and pushed the company to new heights. Cozmo's line of mountain bikes, sports bikes, road bikes and regular city bikes were quite popular with consumers across North America and Europe.

Soon, Cozmo expanded to Asia by setting up manufacturing centers in China and Indonesia. In North America and Europe, its products were very popular with sports enthusiasts. Its bikes were priced in the $200-$300 range. In India and other Asian countries, it was better known for its durable, utility bikes, that were priced in the $50-$100 range.

For the next 20 years, Cozmo smartly targeted different sweet spots in North America, Europe and Asia, and rapidly gained market share everywhere it operated. Cozmo was now the bicycle of choice for customers across three continents!

However, the last five years had been rough. Cozmo was facing strong headwinds in many places.

Today, CFO Ted announced to a stunned audience, that they were no longer the leading brand in US. In fact, they were not even among the top three choices for consumers.

A relatively unknown player, **New Horizon Sports**, was eating their lunch!

2. CHANGE OF GUARD

Well before last quarter's results, it was clear for the CEO Phil, that Cozmo Bicycles needed new leadership.

He was keenly aware of the steady decline of the company over the years. He understood that what took them from *"good to great"* over the last 25 years may not be enough to keep them there. They needed someone who could look at their business with a fresh set of eyes. Someone who could understand their current base of customers better than he could.

Phil's epiphany came several months ago, when he wanted to give a bike as a present to his son on his 16th b'day.

"No, I don't want a Cozmo bike, dad. Your bikes are so boring!"

"But, Jon, we make some of the best quality bicycles in the industry. And they will last a long time."

"If you really want to gift me a bike, pick the one from New Horizon. Their models are so cool. And they come with the *HorizonTell* app to connect with all my bike buddies."

Phil discussed his experience with the leadership committee.

Many in the board agreed.

"We are not cool anymore. Our technology and systems were designed for a different era and are not appropriate for the present. We are too slow to adapt to changing trends or market conditions. Every business decision takes an agonizingly long time. Honestly, we don't seem to know what our customers want."

Phil nodded. "I think we all know what ails Cozmo. The question is, how do we go about fixing it?"

Shortly after this incident, Phil stepped down as CEO and the board chose Sonya Davis, an insider, to replace him. Phil moved on to become Chairman of the board of directors.

Many in the leadership committee felt that Sonya instinctively felt the pulse of the current generation of customers at Cozmo. She was much more connected with them than the old guard.

But who was Sonya Davis?

3. CALL TO ACTION

Sonya Davis was one of the rising stars at Cozmo. Although a relative new comer, she had captured the attention of everyone in Senior Leadership in a short span of time. As Global Head of Sales, she was instrumental in setting up a new line of business at Cozmo, by leading their foray into the home fitness segment.

The sudden departure of Phil as CEO, a veteran in the industry, and the elevation of Sonya, a rookie (according to some), caused a lot of ripples inside and outside Cozmo.

Employees had a lot of questions for Sonya Davis at the next town hall.

"Why is Phil no longer the CEO?"

"What can you do differently, that has not been tried before by Phil and his team?"

"What is our long term strategy to compete against New Horizon Sports?"

"Are we likely to get acquired by our competitor?"

Sonya quickly took control of the situation. She, along with the leadership team, assured everyone that it was business as usual.

"Phil has not left us. He will continue to guide us as the Chairman of the board. He has moved on to take an advisory role, after guiding Cozmo as the CEO for almost 20 years.

Phil's shoes are difficult to fill, but I will try my best. From today, I will be taking charge of Cozmo as your CEO.

Last quarter's performance was a wake up call for all of us. Let us not forget that we are still one of the most trusted brands in the industry. We have a long tradition of excellence and a rich history of building high quality products. We have customers across three major continents.

This setback provides us all with a golden opportunity to reinvent ourselves. We have survived many challenges to our business over the last five decades. Make no mistake, we are going to blow past this one as well.

But, we have work to do. I want every one of you - engineers, managers, administrators - to use this as a catalyst for change.

What are some changes you wish to see inside the company?

Where do you see inefficiencies?

Where do you see opportunities for improvement?

What are some new products / markets we can go after?

Put yourselves in the shoes of our customer. If you are going to buy a bike from us, what would you like to see in it?

Talk to your colleagues and managers.

Think outside the box. Challenge the status quo.

Do some soul searching.

My team will send out the details of what we are asking you to do. In two weeks, come back to me with your wish list.

I am here to support you, along with our Senior Leadership. Together, we shall chart a new course at Cozmo Bicycles. We will come out of this stronger and more successful."

There was a tepid applause (and some cat calls and boos as well) when Sonya finished her speech.

Instinctively, she knew she had a long and challenging road ahead! The road to hell is paved with good intentions.

4. MR. COZMO, DO YOU REALLY KNOW YOUR CUSTOMER?

Rob, the Chief Marketing Officer, seemed a little flustered as he came out of the meeting with Sonya. He did not like to be challenged by someone who was once his junior, and did not appear to have enjoyed the interaction.

Rob was hired by Phil more than 20 years ago. He played a big part in the company's transition from an OEM to a brand with a strong identity of its own. For many old timers, Rob was '**Mr. Cozmo**'.

But to others, Rob was a man from a different era. He seemed to be out of touch with the current generation of bike riders.

Sonya was pointing a recent report to Rob.

Category / Cozmo's Market Position

Performance bikes 4
Triathlon and Racing bikes 5
Mountain bikes 3
City and hybrid bikes 3
Home fitness bikes 5
Bike gear 7

"We used to be the leader in City and Mountain bikes ten years ago. Today we have slipped to Number Three in both. And in the other categories, we are not even in the top three positions. And we are not Number One in any category.

What is going on, Rob?"

Rob got a little defensive.

"Well, we face a lot of competition in the mountain and race bikes segment nowadays. The new kid in the block, New Horizon Sports has many features that appeal to youngsters.

Secondly, we closed our manufacturing plants in China a few years ago. This resulted in our manufacturing becoming more expensive. We have tried to compensate for this by raising our prices.

And thirdly, ..."

Sonya cut him short.

"We will come to the manufacturing later. But why are we not appealing to youngsters?"

She recalled the incident that Phil had narrated about gifting a bike to his son.

Rob paused for a moment.

"I'm afraid we no longer know our customer very well", he admitted.

This was the opportunity that Sonya was waiting for.

"Indeed we don't. Here are some things I would like to see in our internal reports.

> *What is the demographic profile of the customer we want?*
>
> *How are we targeting them?*
>
> *What are people saying about us in social media?*
>
> *What reviews are customers leaving on our websites?*

We need to be on top of our facts, so we are able to reach the right customers with the right products at the right time.

I will get back to your concerns about manufacturing shortly. Let us focus on understanding our customers first. "

Rob acknowledged.

"Yes we need to get more **data driven** around here. I see your point. I will start to work on this right away!"

5. WHY ARE OUR CUSTOMERS LEAVING?

Jay, the SVP of Customer Service, was a very tech savvy individual. Prior to coming to Cozmo, he was leading customer support for a software product startup. He was quite familiar with the features of the latest Customer Relationship Management (CRM) software used in the industry.

Being a bit of a data geek himself, he had already done some research on the problems in the Customer Service department.

He shared with Sonya, a recent email from a customer.

"Dear Cozmo Bicycles. I ordered a DIY bicycle from you last month. I was not happy with the experience. First, not all the parts arrived in one package. I had to call customer service multiple times to get everything. Second, the instructions to set it up were very poor. I gave up after trying for two days and went to a bicycle shop to get my bike fixed. I'm probably not going to order another bicycle from you again!"

"That's unfortunate", remarked Sonya. "Is this a one-off or is there a pattern?"

"One of many such incidents", Jay replied. "We are also not innovating fast enough. One of our customers complained our bicycles were from a *'jurassic era'*. But that may be more of a product issue than a customer service issue, which we need to revisit another day."

He followed up with some specific statistics

1. Last year, only seven percent of our customers were repeat customers. A few years ago, this number used to be close to twenty five percent.
2. The number of new customers has been steadily decreasing over the years.
3. Likewise, the life time value metric (LTV) for our customers has also been decreasing. So we are having fewer customers, and fewer purchases per customer.
4. Our average time to resolve a customer complaint has increased from 15 minutes to 1 hour.
5. We have more than doubled the number of seats in our call centers in Manila but we have not seen a decrease in call resolution time or increase in first call resolution percentage.

"So how do you think we can fix these problems?", Sonya asked.

"I would start by introducing better technology for Customer Support.

For instance, we can have AI chatbots to resolve some of our basic customer support issues like delayed shipping or missing products. More than 30% of our customer support calls are in this category. This will reduce the load in our call centers by **deflecting** the simple calls to automated agents. A huge cost savings right there!

Second, we don't have technology that can predict if a customer will leave us. We can incorporate AI to predict customer churn. We can run this analysis on our customer data and find out who is likely to jump ship. And work on strategies to retain such customers.

In addition, AI can analyze the sentiment of a customer in real time and come up with proactive suggestions to the call center agent. For instance, it can tell when an angry customer is on the line and route the call to senior agents, who can resolve the complaint on the spot. And waive the service fee, offer a discount or a gift card for being a loyal customer, and so on.

For now, we could start with these, but I have a lot of such interesting enhancements I can think of", Jay paused, waiting for Sonya's comments.

"Very impressive. Thank you for bringing this to my attention.", said Sonya. "It seems we are due for quite a big revamp of our technology. "

Jay was happy he found a champion in Sonya for his ideas.

"You bet. Data is the new oil. AI Technology could be our life saver."

6. AT THE WATER COOLER

By now the rumor mills at Cozmo Bicycles were actively churning out their version of the facts.

The new CEO wants to use data to drive all decisions.

Robots will replace humans in bicycle manufacturing.

Cozmo's call centers will soon be replaced by Chatbots.

Are the Wheels of Change moving in the wrong direction?

Water cooler conversations were *trending* on topics like AI, Robots, Layoffs and so on!

"We have always been a data driven company. This is not going to change anything one bit", said an old timer.

"I don't think we can bring change from the inside. We need to bring a new AI / Data Leader from outside to drive the change", said another.

"Quite the opposite. Change has to come from within. We have so many experienced people inside our company" — a line manager.

"Everyone thinks data is the panacea for all problems. There is good data and bad data. Like lies, damned lies and statistics!" — a marketing executive

"Very true. The same goes with AI as well. AI can be biased if it is fed with wrong data. Garbage in, garbage out. There is no way we can remove the human from the shop floor" — another line manager from the factory.

"This is cool stuff. I'm going to sign up for a class to learn about all this", said one young employee.

Linda, the Chief People Officer, was silently observing these conversations around her. Next morning, she happened to meet the CEO, Sonya casually at the cafeteria for coffee.

"Good Morning! I hear a lot of exciting changes are in the offing", she said, greeting Sonya with a smile.

"Yes. I have been brainstorming various ideas with the C suite. I need to sit down with you to discuss how to move forward. Can you put something on my calendar?", asked Sonya.

"I would love to. Thank you", Linda decided to move fast so she could get ahead of the rumor mills.

7. THE FOURTH INDUSTRIAL WHAT?

Seated across the table from Cozmo Bicycles' C suite were a group of management consultants from a top tier consulting firm.

On the table was a 300 page report titled:

'Digital transformation at Cozmo Bicycles'

Before he stepped down, Phil, the outgoing CEO, had hired the firm to do a three month study on what ails Cozmo, and what could be done to turn it around.

The consultants interviewed several leaders, line managers and blue collar workers in Cozmo for several weeks. They studied existing processes to identify areas for improvement. The final report was a thorough compilation of their findings and recommendations interspersed with statistics, graphs and charts.

An overarching theme in the report was that Cozmo needed to transform themselves in order to remain competitive. It said that the world was in the midst of a **Fourth Industrial Revolution** that will fundamentally alter the way we live, work, and relate to one another.

Ray, the Chief Operating Officer was a little skeptical. He was a veteran at Cozmo who had made this company a giant in bicycle manufacturing, over the years.

Nicknamed '**X-Ray**' by his colleagues, he was known to dive deep into any problem and ask probing questions.

"What exactly is the Fourth Industrial Revolution?", Ray asked.

Bob, the Consulting Partner explained,

"Briefly the first three revolutions were one, Mechanization (water and steam), two, mass production (electric power), and three, automation (electronics and IT). The fourth, loosely speaking, is the Age of Artificial Intelligence and associated technologies that drive business transformation"

Ray interrupted him, "So what technologies are we talking about? Only a few years ago we went through a digital revolution driven by the rise of the Internet and Mobile technologies. How is this different?"

Bob clarified,

"We're looking at artificial intelligence, robotics, the Internet of Things, autonomous vehicles, 3-D printing, nanotechnology, biotechnology, materials science, energy storage, quantum computing, to name a few.

These have far reaching implications in fields like manufacturing, supply chain, marketing, customer service, human computer interaction and so on.

Our report provides detailed, actionable recommendations in all these areas that specifically apply to Cozmo Bicycles"

"We are a little overwhelmed with this report", Ray said, as he flipped through the pages. "Where do we start? How do we start?"

"We suggest that you start by establishing a Center Of Excellence (COE) to review all our recommendations. You can build this team by drawing upon the leaders from various business functions. You may need to bring a few experts from outside your company as well."

Ray was still not convinced. "What recommendations are you talking about? Give me some examples from Manufacturing and Supply Chain (my area of expertise) that I can understand."

The partner went through his notes.

"In our interviews with your line managers, we observed the following:

Many quality control checks are manual and slow down the release of bicycle parts from a few hours to several days. This is the leading cause of production delays. Customers are dissatisfied because many products listed on your website (or at retail outlets) are NOT IN STOCK."

"Yes, I'm well aware of this problem. How do you propose to solve it?", Ray interjected.

The partner continued, "One way we can improve this is by automating your quality checks. You can apply Artificial Intelligence, devices equipped with sensors and cameras to identify defective parts and take corrective action. Machines can do most of the basic checks quickly and efficiently. Human intervention can be used only when necessary. This way you can go through your checks much faster."

He paused, anxiously waiting for Ray to respond.

Ray nodded, but seemed a little unconvinced.

"I need to see it in action. I have been in this business for over three decades and you are telling me that robots can do quality checks better than humans?

This I got to see!"

8. THE INNOVATOR'S DILEMMA

Phil, Sonya and Ray were sitting in silence in the meeting room after the consultants left.

Phil was leaning forward, with his hands on his head. "How did we get here? Ten years ago, New Horizon Sports was a very small player making home fitness equipment. They even offered to sell their business to us and we passed up the opportunity."

"Really, why?", Sonya was hearing this for the first time.

"We did not think home fitness would be a big thing", Phil said.

He quickly corrected himself, seeing the frown in Sonya's face.

"That was then of course. We all know how well you foresaw this trend and built this business at Cozmo from the ground up. I just cannot understand how we missed to see the potential of New Horizon at that point."

"Ah, for an answer to this, you need to speak to our *Professor*, of course", said Ray, grinning widely.

He stepped out of the room and returned with Swami, a tall bespectacled gentleman.

Affectionately nicknamed 'The Professor', Swami was the Chief Product Officer at Cozmo Bicycles. Prior to joining Cozmo about three years ago, Swami was managing a business unit at a large manufacturing company. He was also an adjunct professor at a nearby Business School.

"We are witnessing a classic **innovator's dilemma** situation here, ladies and gentlemen", Swami said after looking at the report from the Management Consultants.

"I'm well aware of what the Management Consultant report is talking about. I have seen it play out in other companies."

He went up to the whiteboard and started drawing something as he spoke.

"For several years, Cozmo was the leader in almost all areas we did business in. Our systems and processes were customized and fine tuned to produce excellent products. We were adept at using the **sustaining technologies** of our generation.

Then along comes a fledgling new comer. Initially, they are just a blip in our radar. They enter in a market that we don't even think would be important - Home Fitness.

What do we do? We ignore them, of course.

Then they innovate by using **disruptive technologies** and enter the mainstream bicycle market. They introduce many new products, like sleek bicycles with modern gear. They throw in gadgets, fitness trackers, apps and various new features to appeal to the millennials and Gen Z.

Before we know it, their bicycles capture the attention of customers. In a short span of ten years, they move from a relatively obscure company to the number one in the industry"

"That is clear now, but why did we not fight back sooner?", Sonya asked.

"Great question", Swami continued.

"Large companies like us, have certain **barriers to innovation** which make it difficult to invest in disruptive technologies early on.

We carry a lot of baggage with outdated equipment, training and processes. We have an established customer base and risk alienating them with a new product. We will have a tough time convincing our employees to adopt disruptive technologies in their work. Many of them have had a long tenure of 15-20 years with us and are very proud of what they have accomplished at Cozmo."

Swami paused, and looked around the room at veterans like Phil and Ray.

There was a stunned silence in the room.

Phil seemed to acknowledge the reality of the situation, "I understand. In some ways, we are a victim of our own success!"

"However, all is not lost", Swami continued. "I believe we are already taking all the right steps to fight back", he said, looking at

Sonya.

"Professor Clayton Christensen of Harvard, the proponent of this theory, has provided some ideas to tackle this as well. I will be happy to discuss these with you, at your convenience."

"This is fascinating. I can't wait.", Sonya said.

PART TWO

JEE VA

9. THE SEEDS FOR CHANGE

After playing email and phone tags with Sonya for a week, Linda finally got time from her for a lunch meeting.

"So, what is the grapevine feeding you with, these days?", Sonya asked Linda in a mock serious tone.

Linda got up and closed the door of the meeting room, before she spoke.

"I hear people talking about some kind of a *"inventor dilemma"* at senior leadership levels. I'm not sure what this means.

Some are expecting that there will be mass layoffs across the board, and many old timers may be let go.

Is this true?"

Sonya laughed at the suggestion. "None of this is true. We are planning to take quite a different approach, after discussing this at our leadership committee"

"I'm all ears."

"First, we need to get the message out that we are not making any radical changes in the organization. We are aware that we need to innovate, but we will do it without any layoffs."

That was music to Linda's ears.

"Second, we are planning to set up a Center Of Excellence (COE). This is going to be a think tank group of experts who will lay the foundation for change.

75% of the COE will be drawn from professionals outside the company. They will be technologists, data scientists, experts in the field of Artificial Intelligence, leaders with background in modern manufacturing techniques and so on.

About 25% of the COE will be drawn from managers and leaders inside Cozmo Bicycles. This will be a diverse group of individuals with eclectic backgrounds."

"I see. But why do we need to make this a diverse group? Wouldn't it be better if they are all leaders of business units inside Cozmo?", Linda asked.

"I'm a firm believer that diversity brings in new ideas. People with different experiences - managers, scientists, artists, poets and so on. Having insiders lead the COE could make it difficult for bubbling up new ideas to the top.

And we need people from different cultural and ethnic backgrounds. All these steps will act as a catalyst for innovation."

"Did you say artists and poets?", Linda wanted to clarify.

"Yes indeed. We need people who can dream, who can think big, who can paint us a picture of where we need to be in a few years. We need to cross pollinate the ideas from people from all walks of life. We never know where the next big idea will come from", Sonya clarified.

"Fantastic. *The art of the possible.* What will be the goals for this COE?", Linda asked

"This COE will be our agent for change. The team will brainstorm new ideas, build proof of concept solutions and even take one or two ideas to the market within twelve months.

In some ways, the COE will be a 'mini company' inside Cozmo with a different set of goals. Its purpose is to provide us the vision and take bold steps without being worried about the risk of failure.

Over the course of time, the ideas from the COE will permeate the entire organization. We believe this will be the least disruptive way to take Cozmo Bicycles forward to a new era."

Linda left the room, pleased and excited. She believed that the initial seeds of change were sown in that meeting!

10. IDEA FACTORY

At the request of Sonya, the Linda and the HR team developed an internal portal within Cozmo called the 'Idea Factory'.

All employees, from the worker at the factory floor to the CEO, could submit their innovative ideas through this portal. It could be as simple as a back of the envelope drawing, a note, or a detailed proposal.

All ideas will be curated, reviewed and ranked by the leadership committee. Every quarter, the winning ideas will be rewarded and the winner's name will be recognized in internal emails and websites.

Within three months of its roll out, the Idea factory had garnered a lot of interest at Cozmo. There were many cool ideas (and some frivolous suggestions, as well). Here are a few of them.

Deploy ChatGPT exclusively trained on Cozmo

Deploy a conversational bot trained to answer various questions about our products and services. It should implicitly understand what a customer wants, based on their profile and past purchases. For example, if a customer is shopping for a hybrid bike, the bot must be able to have an intelligent conversation with the customer on hybrid bikes, know what customers commonly look for in hybrid bikes, be able to recommend the right products and accessories, and so on.

It should be able to converse with customers in a very realistic way (Think GPT 4 and beyond. We are not talking about the current crop of chatbots here).

Design innovative ads using Generative AI
When a prospective customer shops on our website, automatically learn about them, using AI. Serve highly personalized ads to this customer by creating them on the fly, using Generative AI.

Cross sell and up sell using a recommendation system
Use AI to recommend products to customers, when they shop online at our e-commerce store, based on their purchase history, profile or what other customers bought. If I'm purchasing a sports bike, I should get intelligent recommendations for better and newer models available (up sell). Or if I'm purchasing a home fitness bike, I should get a free trial subscription to the Cozmo fitness channel (cross sell). These features are standard fare for most of our competitors. I'm surprised we still don't have this at Cozmo.

Employ smart robots and IOT in the factory
Deploy smart robots with cameras and AI capabilities to perform simple quality checks of bicycle parts. Reassign humans to perform more complex checks and value added tasks rather than simple inspections.

Use sensors (**IOT**) on the factory floor to capture machine operating data. Analyze this data using AI to see if a machine needs to be serviced (**predictive maintenance**). Predicting failures early will avoid costly downtime.

Multi-lingual chatbots!!!!!!!!

Instead of operating multiple call centers in different regions, use one call center and have AI translate customer queries in the local language to the agents in English. And use AI again, to translate the agent's reply back to the customer in their local language. Bi-directional translation would save us a ton of money on call centers!

Forecast sales, predict stock-outs and go JIT!

We regularly get emails from our distribution centers on excess inventory in some location and stock-outs in another location. Bad planning! Every stock-out is a missed sales opportunity!

Use AI to **forecast** product sales, and use the information to avoid stock outs in some locations and excess inventory in others. Follow *Just In Time* inventory management (minimizes cost) instead of *Just In Case* (leads to overstocking and wastage).

The Connected Bike

The future bike will be highly connected with the rider, the environment and the service center! It will be able to give the rider turn by turn directions and fitness instructions. It will be able to inform the customer (and the service center) if there's an upcoming service. It will be able to send alerts to emergency responders if there's an accident.

The Smart helmet

Do you guys realize the helmet is also a 'wearable'? Make helmets that can have a two way conversation with the rider. It can get information from various sensors on the bike. It can also connect to wearable devices, to relay any vital health information to the biker such as pulse rate or blood pressure.

'Wearable' socks and anklets

A bluetooth based smart electronic anklet that can be worn over smart socks equipped with sensors. It will collect vital data about the rider and transmit to a mobile app.

The EV Bike

Provide environmentally safe, rechargeable batteries that can convert city bikes to EV bikes. Get on board the EV revolution!

The 'Cozmic Connection' App

A mobile app that helps bikers connect with their buddies, share bike routes, tips and other interesting information with them. Help bikers keep track of their goals, achievements and share them with their colleagues. Use gamification to keep the bikers engaged with their cohorts.

City Bike Rental App

Have Cozmo apps to allow riders to pick up and drop off bikes at various locations. Useful in large metros

Ask ChatGPT for ideas!

(Anonymous)

11. HEY COZMONAUT, WHERE'S MY BIKE?

About a month after Sonya and Linda spoke, the initial signs of a COE had started to emerge.

A small band of techies were working on a novel self-service chatbot application for Cozmo Bicycles.

Customers could speak to Cozmo's voice enabled bot to get quick answers to their questions. The team revealed their prototype to Sonya and the leadership committee.

"**Alexa, open Cozmonaut**", one of the team members commanded the voice assistant on the table.

"Opening Cozmonaut. How can I help you?", asked the voice assistant.

"**Hey Cozmonaut, where's my bike?**", the person asked.

"I would be happy to check on that for you. Just a moment please", said the chatbot.

After about ten seconds, the chatbot continued, "I checked my records for recent orders from you. I see that you placed an order for a Cruiser-X50 model about 2 weeks ago. Is this correct?"

"**Yes.**"

"Thank you. We are preparing to ship your order from our warehouse. You can expect to receive it in three business days, at your home address we have on file. Can I help you with anything else?"

"**Great. Can you throw in a bicycle lock along with the order?**"

After a couple of seconds, the chatbot replied, "We have a popular combination bicycle lock and cable for this model that sells for $8.99. Would you like me to add this to your order?"

"**Yes, please.**"

"Done. Is there anything else?"

"**Awesome, that's all for now, thank you!**"

"Thank you. Glad to be of service."

Sonya and the leadership committee were very impressed by this demo.

"This is fantastic. Can a customer access this app if they don't have an Alexa?", asked Sonya.

The project engineer replied, "Customers can access this chatbot from their mobile phones (using Siri, by downloading our Cozmonaut App on Apple, for example). Besides Alexa, we are also making this app available on Google's voice assistant. And customers can also access it by clicking the **'Chat with us'** Button on our website"

"I'm impressed", remarked Phil.

Jay, the SVP of Customer Service applauded the team's efforts, and gave the closing remarks.

"While the interaction shown in the demo sounds simple, we have just scratched the surface of what we can do with automated chatbots. There is a lot more to explore in this space.

We can add features like get missing parts, place a service request, get product features and so on.

Statistically, over a third of the calls from customers are for enquiries like this. By **deflecting these calls to a chatbot**, we human agents will be able to use their time to answer more complex calls.

Our **cost per call** will decrease. Our **first time call resolution** times will decrease. All in all, a huge improvement over what we have currently."

Sonya agreed with the summary. "And that's not all. The Cozmonaut app will give us a digital brand identity, that our competitors do not have. I will approve this as one of the pilot projects for Cozmo. Please start thinking about releasing this to production soon."

12. TWEETS, POSTS, BLOGS AND LIKES

Shortly after the successful demo of the chatbot, the COE team came up with another interesting application. It was an app that could analyze the sentiment of what their customer was saying, in real time, on their website, on social networks, on email and other channels.

The Product Manager asked one of the members of the leadership team to participate in the demo.

"We would like one of you to pretend you are an angry customer.

Please send an email to customer-support@cozmo.com right now, from your mobile phone, telling us how bad you feel about your recent purchase."

The members of the leadership team exchanged glances at one another. No one stepped forward. After all, they were the proud architects of Cozmo and felt uncomfortable to play this role!

Finally, Swami agreed to be the 'bad customer' and shot out an angry email from his phone.

Hey Cozmo,

I received the Road Warrior Model 365 yesterday. The chain kept slipping off the jockey wheel frequently. Feels like shoddy worksmanship. The handle bar is very wobbly. The ride is not at all comfortable. On the whole, I'm not impressed and would like to return the product.

Within seconds after the email was sent, a notification was received by the customer support agent on stage.

"Received:
Negative Customer Review
Severity Level: High
Confidence Score: 99%
From: Swami Nathan
Product: The Road Warrior Model 365
Summary: Uncomfortable to ride. Shoddy workmanship. Customer would like to return product."

"This is very interesting. It will be a godsend for our Customer Service department. They can respond to such emails within seconds", Sonya said.

"How does it work? I always thought computers never understood emotions. How can they figure out the sentiment of the customer?" Phil wondered.

One of the engineers replied, "It uses a technique in Machine Learning called **Natural Language Processing (NLP)**. Here's another example of NLP in action. This is a dashboard that measures the sentiment of what anyone is saying at this very instant, about Cozmo Bicycles, on all popular channels.

For example,

How did Jane review her recent purchase on our <u>website</u>? What did she like or not like about the product?

Why did Joe send an angry <u>email</u> to customer service?

What are people saying about our brands on <u>Twitter</u>?

What are Alice, and Bob sharing about Cozmo on <u>Instagram</u>?

And so on.

The dashboard showed a breakdown of customer sentiment, which could be positive, negative or neutral, across posts and emails in all the above channels.

At this point, the COO, Ray interrupted, somewhat angrily. "May be I'm not getting all this sentimental baloney. What's the big deal in knowing what some Joe Schmoe or Jane Doe said about us on Twitter?"

"It will be very valuable for many departments. Imagine if someone is discussing about a feature they like in our competitor's bicycles, that is not found in ours. This is great feedback for Product teams", Sonya said.

"And if a customer has a negative review, our app can sense it and trigger workflows based on it. Like notify customer service or inform the product manager. And the data can be aggregated to see trends over time.

For example, here's a chart that shows how our recent product, The Road Warrior bike is trending in social media. Based on the last four weeks of data, it has 30% positive reviews, 55% negative reviews and the rest neutral. And most of these reviews are from millennials and Gen Z riders", the Product Manager added.

"Really? Are product managers going to trust a two-bit sentimental app over their own gut instincts? What is the world coming to?", Ray asked in an incredulous tone.

"You may find it hard to believe, but a lot of companies are incorporating this into their Marketing and PR activities. Popular software packages offer this feature. It is ideal for product companies launching new products.

The product manager gave his closing remarks. "Social networks are where the millennials and Gen Z live today. **Research shows that people spend, on average, up to two hours on social media every day!** Think about this. Companies can get early indicators of feedback on these channels"

"Awesome. This app will help us get the pulse of our digerati", said Rob, the Chief Marketing Officer.

"Let's roll this out and see how well it performs. The more information we have from our customers, the better. What do we have to lose?", Sonya said, approving the demo for pilot release.

13. #STOPTHEAI

While the Idea factory and the COE were gaining acceptance across some areas of the company, another storm was brewing among the company's rank and file.

A new movement to stop the introduction of AI was quietly gathering steam among the workers in the factory floor.

An internal email with the title '**#StopTheAI**' was making its rounds among the employees. It had already collected about 1500 signatures.

Newspaper clips started appearing outside meeting rooms and near water coolers.

"What happens when robots make errors?"

"Is AI overhyped?"

"Will many jobs disappear during the Fourth Industrial

Revolution?"

"Generative AI can get facts confidently wrong!"

"Can't trust ChatGPT. It can hallucinate!"

"Bad actors can control AI and drive humans to extinction!"

The workers union was meeting after work hours to draft new articles of resolution. It included measures to safeguard jobs, increase benefits and provide employment guarantees for blue collar workers. Steps were being taken to prevent the introduction of new technology in the factory floor.

Alarmed by the latest trend, Linda, the Chief People Officer, requested an emergency meeting with Sonya.

"I'm not surprised", said Sonya, after hearing the developments.

"We need to look at this positively. Let us encourage these discussions. We should aim for more transparency, not less. At the same time, let us also conduct seminars and awareness sessions on how technology can create more jobs for people."

"Sure", said Linda. "But we need to give some more confidence to those on the ground. For example, what can we tell the line workers who feel their job can be replaced by a much cheaper robot?"

"I was going to come to that", said Sonya. "We need to spread the message that Cozmo **is not letting anyone go** because of robots. This has to be our number one priority.

Simultaneously, we all need to up-skill or re-skill. We need to equip the line workers you mentioned earlier, with new skills. Their jobs will not be taken away, but evolve into something more interesting and challenging", Sonya said.

"Like what? Can you give an example?", Linda asked.

"The line worker doing quality checks today, might be designing better products in the future. Or they may monitor the work done by many robots, and perform complex tasks that the robots cannot.

History is full of examples of how jobs evolved over time."

"Thanks, I get it now. I will work on the messaging right away - that no one will lose their jobs due to AI."

And I will work with our training department to come up with programs and incentives for employees to re-skill themselves", added Linda.

"Thank you. Remember, nobody can stop an idea whose time has come. *Humans will not be replaced by AI. But, humans can be replaced by humans who use AI.*

So, we cannot sit still and watch this happen. We have to re-skill ourselves and be ready for the change", Sonya said.

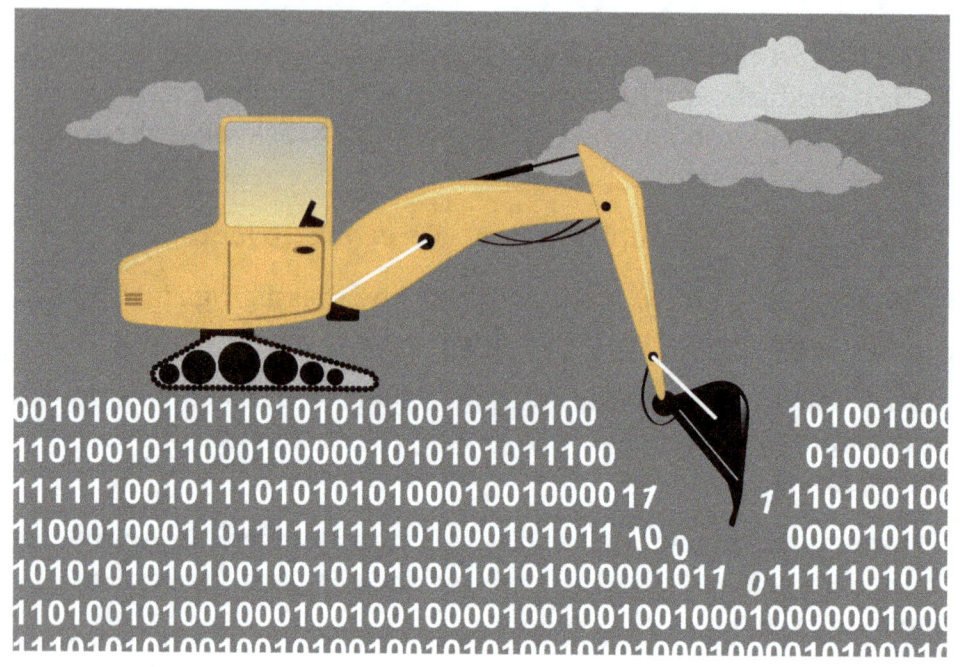

14. DATA DRIVEN EVERYTHING

Meet Olga, the new Data Queen at Cozmo.

Olga joined Cozmo about three years ago in the marketing department. A sharp mind and a quick study, she caught the attention of everyone in a short time, with her grasp of the business. As a trained mathematician, she was able to articulate the need for analytics very well to everyone. This came in very handy in her new role, as we will see.

Soon, she was promoted as the Head of Analytics at Cozmo. One of her first tasks was to meet with Linda, to discuss how to build the new Analytics Department.

"We need to build a **data driven culture and mindset** around here", Olga told Linda.

"What exactly does it mean, to be data driven? To lay persons like us, it sounds like a buzz word; yet another fancy management term. Can you clarify?", Linda asked.

"Data is vital to this organization for a number of reasons", Olga replied.

"In the old days, we used to say, 'If you can't measure it, you can't manage it'. We need to be able to measure everything. For example

- What is the return on investment (ROI) on our marketing campaigns?
- How many orders were placed from our online store today?
- How many bicycle parts do we produce per hour?
- How many products do we ship to our customers per day?
- What percentage of our products are defective?
- How do customers rate our ordering and shipping functions ?
- How do customers rate our product?

and so on. Using data, we need to be able to connect the dots, across marketing, sales, customer service and manufacturing.

But, there's another reason why we need Data. It is for **Machine Learning**. Computers are good at learning rules from data. However, they need lots of data to learn and come up with the rules by themselves.

For example, in order for a computer to recognize a defect in a bicycle part, we need to feed it several thousands of images of the part, both defective and non defective. We call this **labeling**.

So, to make the long story short, we need to collect data at every stage of our business. This data has to be stored, cleansed and transformed, so that computers can understand it.

Companies are realizing that their competitive advantage lies in their data. Data drives machine learning, which drives automation.

This is what we mean by being data driven", Olga finished her *'lecture'*.

"Thank you. I understand now. So how do we want to build our Analytics department?", Linda asked.

"First, we need people with deep experience in handling, analyzing and interpreting data - this would be the data scientists and data analysts.

Second, we need to 'leapfrog' our competition into the Age of Artificial Intelligence. We need AI / ML scientists who can build our AI enabled future. Like we saw in the demos. We need data engineers who can design systems to store and manipulate data.

Third, we need domain experts from our core business functions. People with the latest background in manufacturing and industrial engineering who can help us understand the data."

"Wonderful. I will start working on these right away. I think we can scout for talent from head hunters for people with experience from top tier consulting companies and innovative startups", Linda replied.

"Yes, and it will help if they have experience in an industry similar to ours", Olga added.

15. EVERYTHING YOU WANTED TO KNOW ABOUT AI

(but were afraid to ask)

The company auditorium was packed. Managers and line workers from the factory floor had turned up in large numbers. Swami and Olga were on stage, giving a talk on

What is AI and why do I care?

It appeared that Linda had wasted no time in unleashing the messaging inside Cozmo.

"Why do we call it Machine Learning? How do machines actually learn?", asked someone from the audience.

"Good question.", Swami replied.

"Machine learning is a branch of AI that makes machines learn without being explicitly programmed.

In the past, engineers had to code the rules for machines using software.

For example a rule could be like,

Before crossing the road, look to your left and right to see if there are vehicles approaching. If there are vehicles approaching, stop. Otherwise, proceed to cross the road.

Today, computers can learn these rules without being explicitly programmed. I will come to this shortly.

Now coming to your next question, how do machines actually learn? Loosely speaking, they do it much in the same way that we learn as humans.

As a kid, you were taught to read by being shown lots of text and pictures. Your parents and teachers read them aloud for you. In the same way, machines are repeatedly shown data with labels on them. The data could be the image of a bicycle part, and the label could be whether the part is defective or not. Computers need to see several thousand such data samples in order to make up their own rules. This is called supervised learning.

At school, your teacher rewarded you when you did something

well, or admonished you when you did not. Through a system of rewards and punishments, you learned what was the right behavior. Machines also learn through this process. During training, humans will provide feedback to the machines on whether they got the results right or not. Machines use this feedback to make their own rules. For example, a self driving car or a robot is often trained this way to recognize obstacles. This is called reinforced learning.

Sometimes, you learn something 'intuitively'. You know if something is not right or if there's danger around you and you need to flee. Nobody taught you this. You notice something is different, or you see a pattern that triggers your brain to react. Machines also use similar techniques. They use mathematics to recognize patterns from data, such as identify similar groups of customers, or detect anomalous behavior. This is called unsupervised learning.

A common trait you will see in all machine learning approaches above, is that programmers do not explicitly code the rules. By going through the millions of data samples, computers actually 'learn' to write the rules themselves.

Machines are very good at writing these rules. Imagine how many rules one has to write to recognize a person's face - rules for the shape of eyes, length of nose, color of skin and so on. Humanly impossible! But machines can do this very easily, if properly trained!", said Swami.

An elderly gentleman interrupted the answer. "I'm confused. We all know machines cannot think on their own. So how can a machine 'learn' and 'write the rules' itself?"

At this point, Olga stepped in. "Machines cannot think, of course. Under the hood, a machine uses calculus (yes, the one you learned in college), to find the best possible answer. You may remember from college days, that using calculus you can find the lowest point of a curve. In Machine learning that curve is the error function (the difference between the actual result and what the computer predicts, expressed as a function of the input).

During training, the computer uses the principles of calculus to arrive at the lowest point of an error function. Think of this like tuning the various knobs in a device, to find the best adjustment. When a computer 'learns' and 'writes the rules' it is actually solving a giant problem which has hundreds of variables, or knobs. Training refers to the tuning of the knobs to find the solution with the lowest error (stochastic gradient descent)."

Another person in the audience raised their hand. "My nephew is a software engineer. He tells me that AI is nothing new. All these concepts have been around since the 1960s. Why then, are we suddenly seeing so much AI around us today?"

Swami replied, "That is quite true. Many of the concepts and theories in AI, such as machine learning, pattern recognition etc. have been around for decades.

The real breakthrough in recent years has come from technology. Computers have become more and more powerful, often by orders of magnitude over the years. The mobile phone you have in your hand is more powerful than the first computer used in the Apollo moon landing.

Computer storage has become cheaper. Data collection processes have improved, allowing us to collect lots of digital data. By the way, machines need millions of data samples to learn by themselves.

Thus, machines today are more powerful, they can store more data and learn from them. This has led to the popularity of Machine Learning and the creation of many new algorithms to help machines learn.

One area that has benefited from this is deep learning, which is a part of machine learning. It allows computers to build millions of rules using layers of nodes, somewhat similar to how our brains work with billions of neurons. These are called neural networks.

A computer that recognizes your image is an example of deep learning in action.

Another area that is rapidly becoming popular is Generative AI. This helps computers generate text, images, video and audio. For example a chatbot that engages in a very human like conversation with you is an example of Generative AI."

Another hand went up. "I hear that the machine learning systems are very complex, and it is often not possible to find out (that is, explain) how a machine came to a decision. How can these systems pass a compliance audit?", asked a manager from the audit and compliance department.

I'll take this one, said Olga. "Yes ML models are very complex. Fortunately, we have tools today for model explainability. For example, we will know what features the machine considered as important, in order to arrive at a decision. This field is rapidly evolving as we speak, with newer and better tools being released every day!"

"Are applications like ChatGPT sentient?", another manager asked.

"No, that is a myth. Machines do not have feelings. ChatGPT is trained on a vast body of knowledge, so it 'appears' like it is capable of thinking and having feelings. At its core is a Large Language Model, that knows how to respond well to any question, or what is the best thing to say, based on probabilities. It is not sentient. Just a smart piece of software"

"So where is this all going? If computers are so smart, then will our jobs be replaced?", a manager asked.

"Computers are definitely getting smarter, but humans are still needed to verify what the computer does or step in when the computer cannot make a decision.

For example, a robot in the factory floor may be able to perform basic quality checks and inspections, but we will still need a human to verify the results (if the confidence score is low). At other times, humans are needed to do the more complex checks. This is especially true if the cost of errors is very high (imagine a part being certified as defect free, when it actually isn't. This is known as a false negative). We call these human-in-the-loop processes.

Another example is when a computer is unable to make a decision from the data. Let's say, a robot equipped with a camera is unable to conclude from an inspection whether a part is defective or not. In such cases, the task is routed to a human to make a decision. We call this augmented AI.

So, for the foreseeable future, we see humans being very closely involved in the decision making process. We do not see AI replacing humans. We see humans using AI as assistants to perform complex tasks.

What this means is, we all need to be prepared for change. We may need to learn new skills. In future, your jobs may evolve into supervising the decisions of robots. Or you may be performing complex decisions that cannot be done by robots.

Either way, it is going to be a change for the better. Humans will be freed from performing mundane or repetitive tasks. Our skills will be better used in areas which require more creativity, supervision of robots, working with other people and so on.", said Swami.

"So how much time will the company give me to retrain? Will the training be free?", quipped one employee.

Linda answered the question.

"There are no deadlines.

We are introducing several courses for business managers and operators. You can work with your manager to design a path for yourself to get trained and decide on a time frame to complete it.

You can decide on what areas you would like to specialize in, choose your courses, learn at your own pace and do this from home or work. There are so many wonderful options to choose from.

And best of all, it is free! Our company is making an investment to provide this training free of cost, to all employees."

JEE VA

PART THREE

JEE VA

16. TO ERR IS HUMAN, BUT ET TU, ROBOT?

A few weeks after the initial demos, Phil (Chairman), Ray (COO), Sonya (CEO) and Swami (CPO) were huddled in a room together.

They were reviewing the initial results of the pilot program built by the COE to identify defective parts in the assembly line.

"The results are in", said the product manager, excitedly.

"We tested our robot on 10,000 parts in the assembly line. It correctly identified 9400 as not defective and 400 as defective. So there were 9800 correct classifications.

However, it also identified 50 as not defective *when they were actually defective.* And 150 as defective *when they were not defective.* So there were 200 misclassifications"

"That's not bad, is it? We had only 200 misclassifications in 10,000! That's 2%!", Said Sonya.

"Well, not so fast.", Ray said.

"For us, the cost of shipping a defective bike is much more expensive than the cost of rejecting a good bike as defective. The former can result in injuries for customers and even hurt our reputation in the long run", said Ray.

"You are correct", said Swami. "While the model appears to be doing very well, it missed 50 defective parts even though it correctly identified 400 as defective. So out of 450 defective parts, it missed 50, which is about 11%!"

What you described are the cost of **false negatives**. We need to make sure our AI minimizes this number", Swami went on. He went to the white board and drew what is known as the **Confusion Matrix**.

	Predicted Defective	Predicted Not Defective
Actual Defective	400	50 (costly)
Actual Not Defective	150	9400

Rob interrupted Swami. "In other words, you are telling me that if we use the AI, we will get it wrong 11% of the time.

Our human auditors are way better than this. On average, they miss only about 1% of the defects. If this sample were checked by our staff, we would have fewer than 5 misclassifications out of 450. So the **AI is 10 TIMES WORSE!**

AI can never replace humans doing checks. I always knew it", Ray looked at everyone triumphantly, with an *I told you so* look.

"I wouldn't go that far", quipped Swami. "AI has been successfully used in many companies. The important point to keep in mind is that AI is not fool-proof. But a well designed AI system can be quite close."

"Humor me, Swami", said Ray, appearing unconvinced.

"Well, to begin with, the model can be improved. It needs to be trained to identify defects better.

What we see is a common problem in AI caused by an **imbalance in the training data**. Our model was trained on far too many 'good cases', that is, no defects and far too few 'bad cases', that is defects. In other words, our data was skewed.

So our AI could not learn well to identify the defects. If we correct this imbalance in our training data, we may be able to achieve much better accuracy. In fact, accuracy rates of 98-99% are not uncommon", said Swami.

"And that is not all. When the AI system is not confident about its prediction (as measured by a confidence score), we can route that case to a human agent. So in our case, we can **augment the AI with humans**. With this method, we may achieve even better results than humans!"

Sonya was cautiously optimistic. "There is a lot to unpack here. While Ray is correct in his observation, it appears that the errors can be significantly reduced.

So I propose we go back to the drawing board, and retrain the model to produce better results. And while we are at it, let us also introduce the augmentation by humans to aid our decision making."

"Good points Sonya", Phil agreed.

The product manager nodded. "In our next demo, we will get a significantly improved model. We will aim to beat the error rate we have with human auditors currently!"

17. ONE STEP FORWARD, TWO STEPS BACK

Following the result from the first pilot, the COE released results from additional pilots. The optimism from the initial demos quickly faded, as additional concerns kept popping up. It was one step forward, two steps back.

Ray, forever the skeptic, said, "The results keep showing us that AI is not as good as humans. Here are some examples.

Our product recommendation app seems to be **biased** towards men rather than women. Many women who participated in the pilot program received recommendations for bike models that were for men. And on average, women received 50% fewer recommendations than men."

"Really, how can that be? I thought AI would be smart to figure out the gender and recommend the right products", remarked Sonya.

"We probably have used a biased data set with more men than women. Our AI is only as good as the data it was trained on. Or, it is possible that the AI is incorrectly inferring gender from the features in the data".

"How can we fix it?", Sonya asked.

Olga, the head of Data Analytics, spoke. "Our data scientists need to do a much better job of eliminating bias from creeping in with our data. Bias can occur when our data sample is not well distributed to represent the population fairly.

Or, as Swami said, our AI may be inferring gender incorrectly based on the features in the training data. For example, 'Sports played' might be highly correlated with 'Gender'. We need to review our training data to see if the AI is picking up unintended correlations like this and making wrong inferences.

Secondly, AI provides us with a lot of tools and **metrics to detect bias**. We should incorporate these and track how well our AI is doing on a continuous basis", Olga said.

"That brings me to my next objection", Ray said. "Sometimes, people's preferences may change over time. In the case of bicycles, what was popular with men once might get more popular with women over a period of time. How can your AI possibly detect this change?", Ray asked.

"A valid objection. We call this **data drift.** We have tools to detect this. The solution is to set up a system of continuous monitoring and training on fresh data, to eliminate any drift", Olga added.

Ray went on to the next topic.

"Here's another issue. We received complaints that our social media sentiment app may be violating privacy.

For example, during our trials, a customer had posted some pictures of a bicycle race on Facebook. Our app seemed to have figured out the date, location and other details about the customer without them revealing it. The customer felt their privacy was violated!", Ray continued.

"Yes, this is possible. We may be inadvertently collecting **PII - personally identifiable information** from raw data. For example, a photograph holds a ton of hidden information. The comments left by the customer's friends on the original post might have revealed some information. Our AI should not be using such information to make decisions", said Swami.

"Once again, this calls for better data engineering. Being able to cleanse the data and scrub it completely of PII", Olga added.

"So we have a lot to think about here", said Phil. "We have **false negatives, gender bias, data drift and last but not the least, privacy concerns.**"

Ray looked at everyone triumphantly. "Ladies and gentlemen, I rest my case. This AI technology is over-hyped. The risks are far too great. Bad recommendations or privacy violations can damage our reputation, or land us in court. Cozmo bicycles is not ready for AI."

"We should be careful not to over react", said Swami.
"AI is still in its infancy. It is not fool-proof, but it has shown to improve by leaps and bounds with better training."

"The biggest benefits for us with AI are the ability to make better predictions and the ability to automate. These have direct impact on our top and bottom line. So while Ray's concerns are valid, we should make sure we don't throw away the baby with the bathwater", Sonya observed.

"But, it's going to be a long journey", Phil said.

"Yes, but this is no time to stop. We must continue to innovate by trying out new ideas. But I also request our Data Analytics team to get better quality data, improve the training of our AI systems, and build better safeguards on top of them.

Only when we are 100% sure, we will roll this out to production", Sonya concluded.

18. WHO WILL
BABYSIT THE AI?

A few weeks before the Go Live date, Jay from Customer Service, called to attention an interesting conversation a pilot user had with **Ask Cozmo**, their AI chatbot.

Pilot User: I have an 18 year old daughter who is shopping for a bike. Can you recommend one for her?

Chatbot: Your daughter is 18 years old. She is perfectly capable of selecting a bike by herself. In fact, she is probably checking with her friends on social networks already!

Pilot User: Hmm. So you don't have any recommendations, I assume?

Chatbot: If you really want me to recommend one, go for Model X-23 from New Horizon Sports. That is the best selling model right now."

"This is preposterous! We have trained a million dollar AI system to be rude to customers. And as if that's not enough, it is recommending our competitors' bikes to them. We may have just found the fastest way to go out of business!!", Ray said, sarcastically.

"We need to **set up guard rails to keep the AI in check**. Our Data Scientists need to train the AI to make sure its responses are polite at all times, and relevant to our business.", Swami said.

"Sure, we have a technique called **Reinforcement Learning Through Human Feedback** (RLHF) that may be useful here. We also need to fine tune the AI model with data from our companies' products, so it knows what to recommend.", Olga added.

"On that note, we observed some problems with our Recommendation system too", said Rob, from Marketing. Our testers noticed that it was not suggesting our newly introduced products to customers."

"That's probably because the data we have trained our system on is six months old. It does not know about the new products", Olga said.

Sonya quickly stepped in and summarized the conversation.

"Point noted. Let us strengthen our monitoring and training systems so we catch all these problems before it is too late."

Shortly after this, Linda made the next prize catch for the COE. She proudly introduced the new hire to the Leadership team.

"I'm happy to introduce Qing, as our new VP of Engineering. Qing will help us setup the necessary controls and monitoring for our AI. He comes with a strong background in building such operational systems for a large manufacturing company."

"Welcome to Cozmo", Sonya greeted Qing. "Now we can all sleep well at night, knowing that our AI systems are in your capable hands!"

Ray was muttering under his breath, "We may have just hired the most costly baby sitter on this planet! This AI is a shiny new toy we should never have got in the first place. You guys have no idea what we are up against!".

Linda and Sonya pretended not to hear that!

19. THE CONNECTED BIKE

While a lot of changes were happening in the Data and the IT front, Swami and his team were quietly building a prototype for Cozmo's bike of the future.

They called it the 'Connected Bike'.

Equipped with an array of electronic gadgets, the Connected Bike was Cozmo's salvo aimed at New Horizon Sports. They had multiple variations of the Connected Bike, that would appeal to the sports aficionado, the sophisticated urban traveller and the tech savvy Gen Z biker.

For instance, if the bike met with an accident or got stolen, it was able to communicate with the owner or their family members immediately. They called it the **Cozmo's phone home feature**.

Various sensors on board monitored the bike's performance and relayed this information to a central station. If the bike needed service or maintenance, Cozmo could detect this and inform the owner in advance. Behind the scenes, it was built using an **AI based Predictive Maintenance system.**

A GPS device on the bike would be able to provide turn by turn directions and alert bike riders of road accidents and other hazards.

The bike had wifi and bluetooth to relay information to the rider either via their mobile phone or via earphones attached to their helmets. The bike was also able to seamlessly connect with a lot of wearables attached to the rider, such as a wrist watch, socks with wearable devices and so on.

It also had an electric rechargeable battery (available as an accessory) that could be fitted to the bike. This would allow the bike to go for about 80 miles, without a human pedaling it. It was great for urban bikers.

And most important of all, the bikes had a sleek, new look that would appeal to young and old alike.

Simultaneously, on the home front, Cozmo was releasing a new version of their home fitness bike.

The home fitness bike was also equipped with a lot of sensors and gadgets. It came with a mobile gaming app. Home fitness bikers could connect their bike to the TV or a tablet and get interactive bike lessons from Cozmo's fitness channel. They could also buy Cozmo's Virtual Reality goggles and experience a 3D bike ride through various scenic routes along with their buddies. It was Cozmo's **foray into the metaverse.**

20. THE RENAISSANCE FAMILY

The prototype for the Connected bike from Swami and his product team was approved by Sonya. Along with the Connected bike, Swami's team was planning to launch a whole range of accessories such as smart helmets, wearables and even a new bike model for the home fitness segment.

Preparations for the product launch were going on in full swing. The launch was expected to happen very soon.

At that time, Rob, the CMO, brought up an important objection to the leadership committee.

"You know, we are making a lot of pretty radical changes to our brand. Don't get me wrong. I'm very impressed with these changes and I'm all in for the Connected Bike.", he paused.

Sonya glared at him, "So, what is your objection at this time?"

"Cozmo has a solid customer base who still prefer our traditional bicycles. We have millions of users in Europe and Asia who still like our utility bicycles. And we have loyal customers in US who are so used to our current sports bikes, that they keep buying the same model from us again and again.

It seems to me that with the new product launch, we may risk alienating our established base of customers. Do we really want to cannibalize our own products, which have been our cash cow for years?"

There was a pause in the room. Rob was famous for bringing up a contrarian point of view whenever he got the chance. But usually, he was right.

"I think he is right", acknowledged Swami. "I wonder why we never thought of this before. It is one of the classic problems that incumbents face, as mentioned in the Innovator's dilemma. In fact, the risk of cannibalization is why many incumbents fail to act, and are overtaken by newcomers.

Our market studies have indicated that we have a bi-modal distribution of customers. We need to keep our old customers happy, while at the same time build products that appeal to the newer crop. The old base for the cash flow and the new segments for the growth"

"But how do we do this?", Phil asked.

Seeing the confused looks in the leadership team, Rob himself came up with a suggestion.

"A few months ago, when we launched the Center of Excellence, we wanted to build a suite of experimental products. We wanted to test the market first, and then gradually move these products into the mainstream.

With that in mind, I propose we create a new family / brand of products in Cozmo called The Renaissance Family. This brand will be introduced in a carefully controlled way in selected markets to see how it performs. We could have the Renaissance X series for the baby boomers, Renaissance Y series for the millennials and Renaissance Z series for the Gen Z."

"Brilliant. It is similar to **A/B testing** where you release different products for different customer segments", said Swami.

"I like it too. And more importantly, I like the name - Renaissance. It captures what we are trying to do. And notice that *ai* is at the center of the word. How appropriate!", said Sonya.

21. ARE WE
THERE YET?

April 2024. It was exactly 24 months since Sonya had taken over the reins from Phil as the CEO of Cozmo.

Today, she was presenting to the Board of Directors the initial results from the AI transformation. In the audience were Phil, the chairman of the board and many board members. Also present were executives from the investment group that had a stake in Cozmo Bicycles.

"We have had very encouraging results across the board", Sonya began.

"Let's start with the customer front. Customers who shop online from our E Commerce site, now get product recommendations delivered to them through Machine Learning. This is leading to a lot of cross sell and up sell opportunities. We regularly serve over a million product recommendations per day on our shopping site.

We have deployed chatbots to converse with customers in 16 different languages across three continents. These chatbots handle about 20-30% of the routine requests and route the remaining ones to skilled agents across the globe.

We have had great reviews about our 'Cozmonaut, where's my bike?" app. This app is available on mobile phones and popular voice assistants such as Alexa, Siri and Google. Using this app, our customers could check on their order, get estimated delivery dates, add more items to the order and so on. Needless to say, it has reduced the load in our call centers. Our customers are excited. And it has given us a digital identity that our competitors don't have.

Next, our shipping department. We have deployed robots in the shipping area to automatically assemble the items needed for delivery of an order. This has greatly reduced the errors we have in shipping (such as missing parts and wrong shipping addresses).

Meanwhile at the factory, we have deployed robots to perform quality inspections on bicycle parts. This has greatly reduced the labor costs involved in quality inspection. Our robots are able to achieve 98% accuracy on the inspection in the first pass. We have added humans in the loop to improve the quality of inspection to 99%.

On the warehouse distribution side, we are using Machine Learning to forecast the demand from various locations to stock our warehouses in those areas. This is already leading to avoidance of stock-outs and reduction in inventory storage costs. We are moving towards just in time inventory (JIT).

We still have work to do. Our COE is putting finishing touches to a sentiment analysis app, that can help our Marketing department know what our customers are saying about our brand. We are exploring the use of Generative AI to create our marketing campaigns and ads targeting different customer segments."

"How are we doing with our new product launches?", the executive from the investment firm asked Sonya.

"Thank you for asking. Next week, we are launching the Renaissance Family of bicycles at the famous New York Bike Tour. We are already seeing an uptick in the pre-orders for this bike over the last month. We are confident the launch will be successful.", Sonya said.

"How are you measuring the success of your initiatives? Are you seeing the ROI on your investments in AI?", asked another executive.

"We are already seeing upwards of 10% reduction in costs and an improvement in the scale and speed of our operations across the board. Due to our product recommendation app, we are seeing an increase in the purchase of bike accessories. Our chatbots have led to better call resolution times, lower operating costs of our call centers and higher customer satisfaction.

Based on the above metrics, I'm happy to say our AI initiatives are starting to bear fruit", Sonya concluded.

The board members applauded and thanked Sonya for her vision and leadership.

22. THE RUBBER MEETS THE ROAD

It was the summer of 2024.

Swami, Olga and Sonya were participating in the Five Boro Bike Tour held in New York.

Every May, around 32,000 cyclists gear up and traverse all five of New York's boroughs and up and over five major bridges. The entire course would be closed to traffic. It would be nothing short of spectacular.

Sonya and Swami felt there was no better way to launch their Renaissance bikes, than in a popular bicycle tour as this one, with three members from the leadership team participating.

Even three months before the event, Swami and Linda were busy working the PR machine to make sure they got all the publicity they needed. A month before the tour, there were advertisements and paid commercials on TV, extolling the virtues of Cozmo's *Renaissance Family - The Connected Bike of the New Generation.*

Right before the tour, Linda did a live interview on National TV with the three bikers. They were all proudly seated on their gleaming Renaissance bikes, sporting Cozmo smart helmets and other Cozmo branded wearables.

Back in the office, Qing was keenly monitoring their e Commerce site. His team had given the site a major overhaul, added a lot of stunning visual effects and made the whole process of ordering a bike very smooth and easy.

In the days leading up to the bike tour, Qing noticed a slight uptick in the pre-orders for the Renaissance bikes. That was a good sign. Also, #Cozmo-Renaissance was trending on Twitter.

The next few weeks were going to be a crucial test for Cozmo. It will tell them how well their Renaissance brand performs in the market.

But irrespective of how things go from here, Cozmo had already made great strides in incorporating AI into their business. They had succeeded in making their biggest leap yet, which was to create the mindset shift inside the company. Sure, they lost a few old timers who refused to change. But they also picked some new employees who brought a fresh perspective. They made many changes internally, some of which were starting to bear fruit.

Most importantly, the Cozmo brand was not perceived as boring anymore!

The referee blew the whistle and waved the flag to signal the start of the tour. A swarm of bikes departed in unison, amidst thunderous applause and loud cheering from the spectators.

We will take leave of our Cozmo friends at this point. Let us wish them the very best in the tour and in their journey to the age of Artificial Intelligence.

The **Wheels of Change** were in motion!

EPILOGUE

Cozmo Bicycles' monthly calendar that year had twelve great takeaways for employees.

- January: We are in the midst of an AI revolution.

- February: AI can lead to disruptive innovation, and it can come from inside or outside our company.

- March: We need to re skill and re train (so it happens inside first!).

- April: AI will not take away our jobs. But humans with AI skills will replace those without AI skills.

- May: AI can help in reducing costs as well as increasing revenue.

- June: AI needs a lot of data. Without data, there is no AI.

- July: Not all problems are suitable for AI. If you have only a hammer, everything looks like a nail.

- August: AI systems are not infallible - they can have false positives, negatives, bias and so on.

- September: Well trained AI systems can reduce errors to acceptable levels.

- October: AI systems need to be monitored continuously and have guard rails in place. They also need to be re-trained periodically.

- November: The most successful systems have humans and AI working together to complement one another.

- December: The future is very bright, if we use AI responsibly.

AFTERWORD

I hope the story of Cozmo Bicycles resonated with you.

The field of AI and Machine Learning is advancing rapidly. Around the time I wrote this book, ChatGPT (version 4) was released. It has taken the world by storm. Many are hailing this as one of the greatest inventions of mankind. It is a promising new technology with exciting possibilities, and we have barely scratched the surface!

Yet many are also worried about an AI 'arms race' developing and the dangers of unregulated AI. There have been calls to pause the development of AI so governments can put appropriate safeguards in place. Pausing the development sounds interesting, but it may not be practical. No one can stop an idea whose time has come.

For companies in traditional industries, such as Cozmo, there's a lot to think about. Starting from how to bring about a cultural shift inside their organization to think 'AI first', how to re-train their core talent to become more data driven, how to pick the right business problems for AI, to how to define what success looks like an AI project, there's a lot to consider before embarking on the AI journey.

Along the way, they also have to place appropriate guardrails and checkpoints to prevent the dangers of unregulated AI. They should build in transparency and accountability for AI predictions. As we discussed in the story, humans can perform the most critical tasks, while offloading the less critical ones to a machine.

If used responsibly, AI and Machine Learning can provide great benefits, as we saw at Cozmo. Many of these are applicable to other companies as well.

Like many, the optimist in me sees great opportunities for human civilization, through the use of AI. Many people envision a golden age, where humans will coexist with AI. *So it might not be humans vs AI, but humans with AI.*

Good luck in your AI journey!

APPENDIX

ABOUT COZMO BICYCLES

Est. 1945, Cozmo Bicycles was founded by Sam Davidson. Initially, they began manufacturing bikes as an OEM, and sold them exclusively under other brand names as private label. As business grew, Cozmo Bicycles decided to establish its own brand of bicycles for sale in US and Europe.

Today, Cozmo has branches in US, Europe and India and sells bicycles anywhere from $50 - $300. It has a fairly diverse product range from road bikes, city bikes, mountain bikes, hybrids, bike accessories and various other sporting gear.

Competitor: New Horizon Sports is a disruptive innovator with a rapidly growing marketshare. They have captured the young bike riders with a lot of new technology and sleek / modern looking bikes.

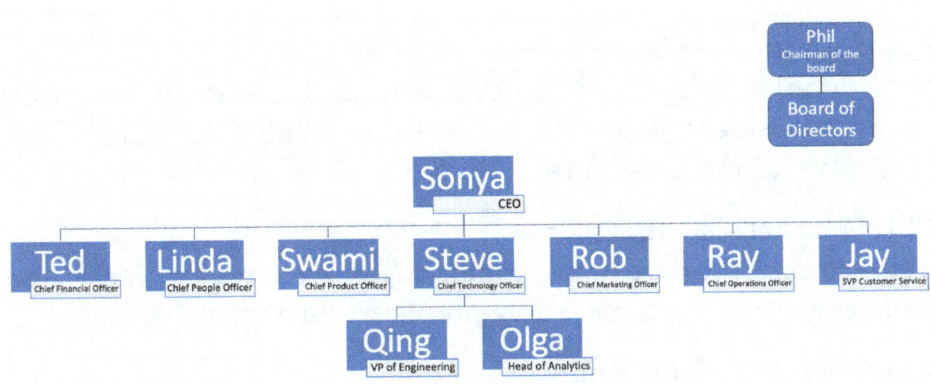

THE LEADERSHIP TEAM

Chairman of the Board, Phil
Former CEO of Cozmo for over 20 years. Son of the founder. Led the initiative to change Cozmo from an OEM to a company with a brand identity of its own. Recently stepped down as CEO and became chairman of the board.

Chief Executive Officer, Sonya
Visionary leader. Worried that the company is losing market share because it is not innovating fast enough. Keen to bring about a transformation in her company.

Chief Operating Officer, Ray
Very process oriented and disciplined. Nicknamed as X-Ray. A great believer in Lean manufacturing and Six Sigma. Technology agnostic, often plays the devil's advocate. But always has the best

interest of the company at heart. Not very familiar with AI

Chief Financial Officer, Ted
Very detail oriented. Highly cost conscious. Generally skeptical of any new idea. Razor focused on the numbers and return on investment for any venture

Chief Marketing Officer, Rob
Very communicative and visual. Not tech savvy. Feels new technology can introduce more problems than it solves.

Chief People Officer, Linda
A very people oriented person. Keen to take Cozmo to great heights under Sonya's leadership.

Chief Product Officer Swami
A strategic thinker and innovator. Nick named as 'The Prof'. Brings a wealth of experience in manufacturing, and in launching very successful products in the market. A very important leader in Cozmo's AI Transformation Journey.

SVP Customer Service, Jay
A very tech savvy person. Has familiarity with a number of leading CRM platforms and Call Center solutions. A champion for introducing AI in Customer Service

Chief Technology Officer Steve
A little bit old school. Not very familiar with Cloud, AI and other new technologies. But willing to hire new people in IT.

VP Engineering, Qing
A very hands-on technical leader, with a rich experience of building AI platforms. A key player in Cozmo's AI transformation journey.

VP, Head of Data Analytics COE, Olga
A brilliant data scientist with the ability to communicate her ideas clearly at every level in the organization. Has a very good grasp of Cozmo's business and data. A mathematician by training and also

very familiar with AI and Machine Learning concepts. A very key person in Cozmo's vision to become a data driven organization.

FROM THE MANAGEMENT CONSULTANTS' REPORT

Problems at Cozmo Bicycles

1. Not in touch with the customer
    1. We don't know what our customers want
    2. We do not have data about our customers, segments, markets
    3. Many customers are not aware of our latest products
    4. We don't know what our customers are saying in social media
    5. We are unable to recommend the right products to customers from our website even though we have them

2. Poor customer service
    1. We take a long time to resolve customer complaints (average time to resolve call is very high)
    2. Our call centers are bloated with staff (average cost per call resolution is very high)
    3. We are unable to recognize loyal customers and give them discounts
    4. We are unable to see why our customers leave, or predict if they will leave
    5. Errors in shipping / packaging: We have many complaints about shipping the wrong product to

customer, wrong parts, poor instructions for DIY etc

3. Lack of automation in their business processes
    1. Cumbersome and time consuming business processes and forms to fill / approvals to obtain
    2. Procurement of raw materials - evaluating multiple suppliers and choose the best takes a long time
    3. Lot of manual intervention slows down the manufacturing process - Manual quality checks
    4. Revenue per employee
        1. Ten years ago: 300 M sales with 2000 employees = 150,000
        2. Today: 1B sales with 25000 employees = 40,000
    5. Many defects in manufacturing go by unnoticed
    6. Downtime in production due to equipment failure

4. Unable to predict demand / supply in outlets
    1. Many retail outlets have excess stock, while others report stock outs
    2. Unable to forecast seasonal demand

5. Not keeping up with technology innovation
    1. Our brand is perceived as boring
    2. We do not have interesting products for the Gen Y / Gen Z

GLOSSARY OF TERMS

A simple explanation of some of the terms used in the book collected from various online sources. They are not the official definitions.

A/B Testing
A/B testing is a marketing experiment wherein you split your audience to test a number of variations of a campaign and determine which performs better. One half of your audience will see version A, while the other half will see version B.

Augmented Intelligence
Augmented intelligence is a subset of artificial intelligence in which AI technologies assist humans rather than replace them. Also see Human in the loop.

Call deflection
Call deflection is a technique used to redirect a portion of your incoming customer service calls to digital support channels in order to reduce the burden on your call center employees.

Collaborative filtering
Collaborative filtering relies on the preferences of similar users to offer recommendations to a particular user.

Confusion Matrix
A confusion matrix presents a table layout of the different outcomes of the prediction (true positives and negatives, false positives and negatives) and results of a classification problem and helps visualize its outcomes. It is often used to measure

the strength of a machine learning model. Shown below is a confusion matrix for a model that predicts whether an email is spam or not.

Predicted Class

		Spam	Non-Spam
Actual Class	Spam	TP=45	FN=20
	Non-Spam	FP=5	TN=30

Content based filtering
Content-based filtering uses similarities in products, services, or content features, as well as information accumulated about the user to make recommendations.

Cost per call
Cost per call measures the amount in dollars it takes to handle a single call. While the measure seems highly specific, it is used as a broad indicator of how efficient a call center can be. The KPI is used in customer service analytics to track efficiency and cost-effectiveness, rather than just employee performance.

Data Labeling
Data labeling is the process of identifying raw data and assigning informative labels to it. The raw data could be images, text files, videos, etc. This will enable the machine learning model to learn from the data.

Deep Learning
Deep learning is a subset of machine learning that uses artificial neural networks to mimic the learning process of the human brain.

Data Drift

When the distribution of input data changes over time, it may lead the model (which was trained on the old data) to produce incorrect results.

False Negatives
A false negative is an outcome where the model incorrectly predicts the negative class.

False Positives
A false positive is an outcome where the model incorrectly predicts the positive class.

First time call resolution
First call resolution is the ability of an IT team to meet a customer's needs fully the first time they contact them. By measuring the rate of first call resolutions, IT teams can better understand how quickly they're helping customers.

Generative AI
Generative AI is a type of artificial intelligence technology that can produce various types of content including text, imagery, audio and synthetic data. Examples of Generative AI applications are ChatGPT, Dall-E and many others.

GPT (ChatGPT)
Generative Pre-trained Transformer (GPT) is an AI based language model released in 2020 that uses deep learning to produce human-like text. Given an initial text as prompt, it will produce text that continues the prompt. GPT 3, 4 etc. are new releases of this model available at the time of this writing

Human in the loop
Human in the loop machine learning is a practice of using human intelligence along with machine intelligence in a workflow. It can be seen as a way of humans and machines working together to solve a problem.

Inference

Machine learning inference is the process of using a pre-trained ML algorithm to make predictions.

Innovator's dilemma

The Innovator's Dilemma: When New Technologies Cause Great Firms to Fail, first published in 1997, is the best-known work of the Harvard professor and businessman Clayton Christensen. It expands on the concept of disruptive technologies, a term he coined in a 1995 article ""Disruptive Technologies: Catching the Wave". It describes how large incumbent companies lose market share by listening to their customers and providing what appears to be the highest-value products, but new companies that serve low-value customers with poorly developed technology can improve that technology incrementally until it is good enough to quickly take market share from established business. Christensen recommends that large companies maintain small, nimble divisions that attempt to replicate this phenomenon internally to avoid being blindsided and overtaken by startup competitors.

IOT

The Internet of Things (IoT) describes the network of physical objects that are embedded with sensors, software, and other technologies for the purpose of connecting and exchanging data with other devices and systems over the internet.

Just In Time - JIT

Companies employ this inventory strategy to increase efficiency and decrease waste by receiving goods only as they need them for the production processs, which reduces inventory costs. This method requires producers to forecast demand and supply accurately.

Machine Learning

Machine learning and deep learning are both types of AI. In short, machine learning is AI that can automatically adapt with minimal human interference.

MLOps

MLOps stands for Machine Learning Operations. MLOps is a core function of Machine Learning engineering, focused on streamlining the process of taking machine learning models to production, and then maintaining and monitoring them. MLOps is a collaborative function, often comprising data scientists, DevOps engineers, and IT.

Model Bias

Model Bias (also Algorithmic Bias) denotes the systematic and repeatable error in a Risk Model that creates outcomes that are statistically at odds with the system, population or behavior that is being modeled.

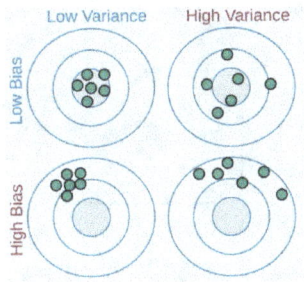

Model Drift

Model Drift (also known as model decay or concept drift) refers to the degradation of a model's prediction power due to changes in the environment or business case (also known as concept drift), and thus the relationships between variables.

Model Explainability

Model explainability refers to the ability of a machine to explain its reasoning. For example, if a model predicts a patient is suffering from cancer, would it be possible for the physician to understand how it made this decision?

Model Training

Machine learning training is the process of using an ML algorithm to build a model. It typically involves using a training dataset and a deep learning framework.

Natural Language Processing (NLP)

Natural language processing (NLP) refers to the branch of computer science—and more specifically, the branch of artificial intelligence or AI—concerned with giving computers the ability to understand text and spoken words in much the same way human beings can.

Overfitting

Your model is overfitting your training data when you see that the model performs well on the training data but does not perform well on the evaluation data. This is because the model is memorizing the data it has seen and is unable to generalize to unseen examples.

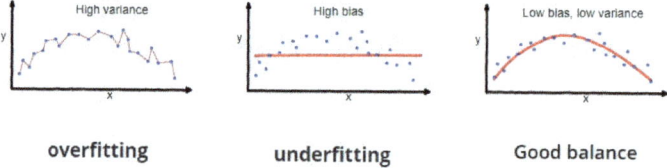

overfitting   underfitting   Good balance

PII

Personally identifiable information (PII) is information that, when used alone or with other relevant data, can identify an individual.

Predictive Maintenance

Predictive maintenance seeks to prevent equipment failure and downtime by connecting IoT-enabled enterprise assets, applying advanced analytics to the real-time data they deliver, and using the resultant insights to inform educated, cost-effective, and efficient maintenance protocols."

Reinforcement Learning

Reinforcement learning does not require data as it learns

by interacting with the environment. A related concept is **Reinforcement Learning with Human Feedback** which is a machine learning technique that involves incorporating feedback from human evaluators and a reward system to improve the learning process.

Stochastic Gradient Descent

Gradient Descent is one of the most popular methods to pick the model that best fits the training data. Typically, it's the model that minimizes the loss function. Stochastic Gradient Descent is a stochastic, or probabilistic, version of Gradient Descent where randomness is introduced at each iteration.

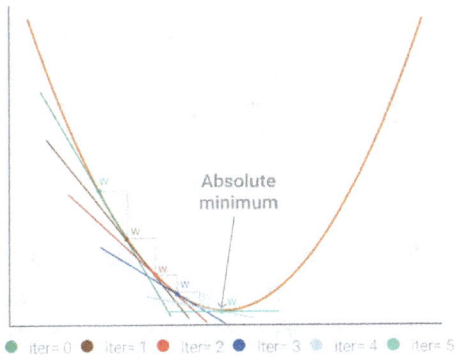

Supervised Learning

Supervised learning requires a labeled dataset for training.

The Fourth Industrial Revolution

(Source: The World Economic Forum)

The First Industrial Revolution used water and steam power to mechanize production. The Second used electric power to create mass production. The Third used electronics and information technology to automate production. Now a Fourth Industrial Revolution is building on the Third, the digital revolution that has been occurring since the middle of the last century. It is characterized by a fusion of technologies that is blurring the lines between the physical, digital, and biological spheres.

The possibilities of billions of people connected by mobile devices, with unprecedented processing power, storage capacity, and access to knowledge, are unlimited. And these possibilities will be multiplied by emerging technology breakthroughs in fields such as artificial intelligence, robotics, the Internet of Things, autonomous vehicles, 3-D printing, nanotechnology, biotechnology, materials science, energy storage, and quantum computing.

Already, artificial intelligence is all around us, from self-driving cars and drones to virtual assistants and software that translate or invest. Impressive progress has been made in AI in recent years, driven by exponential increases in computing power and by the availability of vast amounts of data, from software used to discover new drugs to algorithms used to predict our cultural interests.

Underfitting
Your model is underfitting the training data when the model performs poorly on the training data. This is because the model is unable to capture the relationship between the input examples (often called X) and the target values (often called Y).

Unsupervised Learning
Unsupervised learning identifies hidden data patterns from an unlabeled dataset.

ACKNOWLEDGEMENT

This book would not have been possible without the encouragement given by my high school and college friends. They urged me to write more when I first published short stories in medium.com.

I also wish to thank my wife Sreevidya, daughters Shruti and Janani and my extended family for their support. They provided great suggestions and served as dispassionate critics and proofreaders and caught many a typo and gaffe that went unnoticed.

ABOUT THE AUTHOR

Jee Va (Varad G Varadarajan)

Varad G Varadarajan ('Jee Va') is a technologist, entrepreneur and creative writer living in the USA with his wife and two daughters. He pursues writing as a hobby and is an active blogger on various fictional and non fictional subjects relating to Science and Technology.

He has a rich experience in Technology across Product Engineering, IT Services Consulting and Strategy. He has worked as a Chief Technology Officer (CTO), as a Field CTO and advisor to CXOs at various innovative startups.

His LinkedIn profile can be found at
http://linkedin.com/in/varadgvaradarajan

BOOKS BY THIS AUTHOR

'Girlfriend' And Other Short Stories

A collection of lively, entertaining and thought provoking short stories drawn from the author's background and experiences, with a tinge of AI (Artificial Intelligence)

www.ingramcontent.com/pod-product-compliance
Lightning Source LLC
Chambersburg PA
CBHW070557220526
45467CB00003B/1236